APPLEWOOD's
PICTORIAL AMERICA

HALLOWEEN

APPLEWOOD BOOKS
Bedford, Massachusetts

HALLOWEEN

Copyright © 2009 Olde Yankee Map and Photo Shoppe

For prints of images in this book visit:
www.libraryimages.net/holidays/halloween

Thank you for purchasing an Applewood book.
Applewood reprints America's lively classics —
books from the past that are still of interest to
modern readers. For a free copy of our current
catalog, please write to Applewood Books,
P. O. Box 365, Bedford, MA 01730.
www.awb.com
www.pictorialamerica.com

ISBN 978-1-4290-9707-9

PRINTED IN THE U.S.A.

TABLE OF
Contents

[*N⁰·* 1 FALL: THE HARVEST OF PUMPKINS.]

[*N⁰·* 2 THE HALLOWEEN TRADITION BEGAN AS A
CELEBRATION OF THE ANNUAL HARVEST.]

[*N⁰.* 3   OCTOBER 31ˢᵀ WAS CONSIDERED THE LAST DAY OF
SUMMER IN ANCIENT TIMES.]

[*N⁰.* 4   ALSO KNOWN AS 'SAMHAIN,' HALLOWEEN FALLS ON
THE EVE OF THE CELTIC NEW YEAR.]

[*No.* 5 THE WORD HALLOWEEN WAS ORIGINATED BY THE CATHOLIC CHURCH, WHICH CALLED IT 'ALL HALLOWS EVE.' NOVEMBER 1ST IS 'ALL SAINTS DAY' FOR CATHOLICS.]

[*No.* 6   NOVEMBER 2ND IS 'ALL SOULS DAY' IN MEXICO,
SPAIN, AND LATIN AMERICA.]

[*Nᵒ·* 7 THE TRADITION OF CARVING PUMPKINS ORIGINATED FROM THE IRISH LEGEND OF 'STINGY JACK.' JACK WAS DOOMED TO WANDER ENDLESSLY THROUGH THE DARK NIGHTS WITH ONLY A BURNING COAL EMBER IN A TURNIP (THAT HAD BEEN HALLOWED OUT) FOR LIGHT.]

216   JACK-O'-LANTERN

[*No.* 8 PEOPLE WOULD CARVE SCARY FACES INTO TURNIPS
       OR POTATOES AND PLACE THEM IN WINDOWS TO KEEP
       'JACK OF THE LANTERN' AWAY.]

16023. Gathering in the pumpkins in the Yakima Valley, Wash.

[*N⁰·* 9 BY THE MID-1800s, IRISH IMMIGRANTS ARRIVING IN THE U.S. BEGAN USING NATIVE PUMPKINS RATHER THAN TURNIPS BECAUSE THEY WERE MORE PLENTIFUL THERE.]

[*Nº.* 10   HALLOWEEN LEGEND STATES THAT NOCTURNAL BATS AND
OWLS, AS WELL AS BLACK CATS, ARE OMENS OF BAD LUCK.]

[*Nº.* 11   IT WAS BELIEVED THAT OWLS WOULD SWOOP DOWN ON
HALLOWEEN NIGHT AND EAT THE SOULS OF THE DYING.]

[*N⁰·* 12 THE CELTS BELIEVED THAT THE LIVING AND DEAD
CAME TOGETHER ON HALLOWEEN AND THAT
SPIRITS SOMETIMES CAUSED MISCHIEF AND
TROUBLE, DAMAGING CROPS.]

[*N⁰·* 13 PEOPLE WOULD LEAVE OUT FOOD AND LIGHT HUGE BONFIRES
OF BURNING CROPS TO TRY AND DRIVE AWAY THE EVIL SPIRITS.]

[*N⁰·* 14–15   IN EARLY COLONIAL TIMES, THERE WAS NO HALLOWEEN TRADITION. RATHER, WITCHES WERE PERSECUTED BECAUSE OF THE BELIEF THEY HAD SPIRITUAL POWERS THAT COULD BRING HARM TO THE COMMUNITY.]

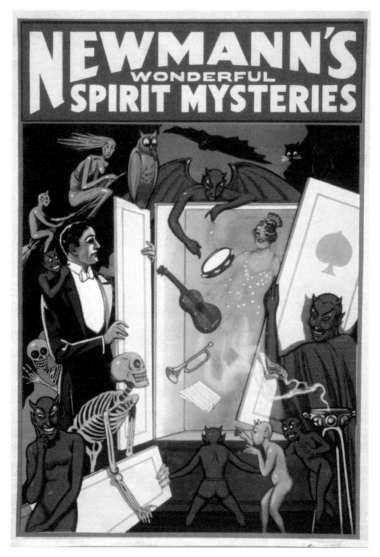

[*N⁰·* 16   RELIGIOUS FEARS ULTIMATELY GAVE RISE TO COMMERCIAL OPPORTUNITY. MAGICIANS EXPLOITED THE CURIOSITIES OF SPIRITUAL MYSTERY .]

[*Nº* 17 THEATER: A WITCH AND EVIL SPIRITS ARE
DEPICTED IN A PRODUCTION FROM 1870.]

[*Nº·* 18   LITERATURE: A DRAWING OF THE WITCH IN THE
CASTLE FROM THE STORY "SLEEPING BEAUTY."]

[*Nº.* 19 MUSICAL: THE SCARECROW AND THE WICKED
WITCH EVOKE TRADITIONAL HALLOWEEN THEMES
IN THE "WIZARD OF OZ," 1903.]

The Witch House, Salem, Mass.

[*Nᵒ·* 20   TOURISM: THE WITCH HOUSE AT SALEM, MASS., 1902.]

HAUNTED CASTLE.

[*Nᵒ·* 21   PRINTMAKING: A HAUNTED CASTLE DEPICTED BY
        CURRIER & IVES.]

[*Nº* 22 THE BLENDING OF CULTURES—WITCHES BEGIN TO
APPEAR IN THE HALLOWEEN TRADITION.]

[*Nº. 23*   IT WAS THOUGHT THAT WITCHES CAST SPELLS,
COMMUNED WITH BLACK CATS, AND CONSORTED
WITH THE DEVIL.]

[*Nº. 24*   THESE THEMES WERE DEPICTED IN THE MANY
POSTCARDS EXCHANGED ON HALLOWEEN AT THE
BEGINNING OF THE 20TH CENTURY.]

[*N⁰·* 25 HALLOWEEN POSTCARD.]

[*N⁰·* 26 HALLOWEEN POSTCARD.]

[*N⁰.* 27 HALLOWEEN POSTCARD.]

Hallowe'en Greetings.

[*N⁰.* 28 HALLOWEEN POSTCARD.]

[*N⁰·* 29 HALLOWEEN POSTCARD.]

[*Nº.* 30 ONE SUPERSTITION HELD THAT IF A BAT FLEW
AROUND A HOUSE THREE TIMES ON HALLOWEEN,
DEATH WOULD SOON COME.]

[*Nº. 31* BATS WERE ALSO THOUGHT TO INDICATE THE
PRESENCE OF GHOSTS.]

[*Nº. 32* GHOSTS WERE COMMONLY THOUGHT TO
REPRESENT SPIRITS OF THE DECEASED.]

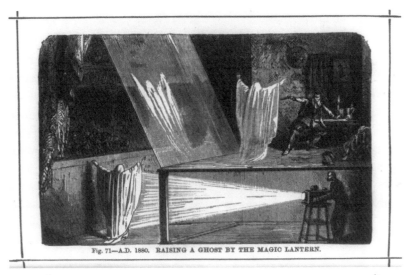

Fig. 71—A.D. 1880. RAISING A GHOST BY THE MAGIC LANTERN.

[*Nº.* 33 GHOSTS AS PORTRAYED IN EARLY THEATER.]

[*Nº.* 34 HOUDINI 'TALKING' WITH THE GHOST OF LINCOLN.]

[*N⁰.* 35 HALLOWEEN POSTCARD.]

⌈ *N⁰·* 36 HALLOWEEN INCLUDED THE BELIEF THAT ON
OCTOBER 31ˢᵀ SPIRITS OF DEPARTED LOVED ONES
WERE ABLE TO CROSS THROUGH THE VEIL THAT
SEPARATES THE LIVING FROM THE DEAD. ⌉

Hallowe'en

Carry a Black Cat in a Pumpkin Shell
And a White Owl on your Right Shoulder
Of the Witches and Goblins you break the Spell
And your Sweetheart's Love will not Moulder.

H 13

[*Nº* 37   ON HALLOWEEN, YOUNG WOMEN BELIEVED THEY
COULD LEARN ABOUT THEIR FUTURE HUSBANDS BY
PERFORMING CERTAIN RITUALS OR PLAYING TRICKS
WITH YARN, APPLE SHAVINGS, OR MIRRORS.]

[*Nº.* 39 YOUNG WOMEN WERE FREQUENTLY TOLD THAT IF
THEY GAZED INTO MIRRORS, THE FACE OF THEIR
FUTURE HUSBANDS WOULD APPEAR.]

A Happy Future
I Hope You will See,
On Hallowe'en in a Cup of Tea.

A
GREETING
for
HALLOWE'EN

[*Nº* 40 HOWEVER, IF A SKULL APPEARED, THEY WOULD BE
DESTINED TO DIE BEFORE MARRIAGE.]

[*Nᵒ.* 41 HALLOWEEN POSTCARD.]

[*N°.* 43 BY THE 1900s, A MOVEMENT BEGAN TO HELP SHIFT THE EMPHASIS ON SPIRITUAL RITUALS TO COMMUNAL CELEBRATION. BOBBING FOR APPLES BECAME A POPULAR GAME.]

[*N⁰.* 44 CHILDREN BOBBING FOR APPLES.]

[*N⁰.* 45 CARVING A JACK-O'-LANTERN.]

[*No.* 46 HALLOWEEN POSTCARD.]

[*N⁰·* 47 HALLOWEEN POSTCARD.]

[*N⁰·* 49 **WWI POSTER.**]

Hallowe'en Pranks

Halloween is sure to be
Tonight your love you shall see.

[*No.* 50 TAKING THE PLACE OF RELIGIOUS SPIRITS, CHILDREN
OFTEN COMMITTED PRANKS ON HALLOWEEN.]

[*N⁰.* 51 IN 1920, ANOKA, MINNESOTA, WAS THE FIRST CITY
IN AMERICA TO OFFICIALLY HOLD A HALLOWEEN
CELEBRATION. THE GOAL WAS TO DIVERT CHILDREN
FROM PERFORMING PRANKS LIKE TIPPING OUTHOUSES
OR LETTING COWS RUN LOOSE ON MAIN STREET.]

[*N⁰.* 52   PRANKSTERS ON HALLOWEEN.]

[*No.* 53 TREATS OF POPCORN, PEANUTS, AND CANDY WERE
OFFERED TO CHILDREN WHO PARTICIPATED IN THE PARADE,
AND IN THE EVENING A HUGE BONFIRE WAS HELD.]

HALLOWEEN

[*Nº. 54* THE EARLIEST KNOWN PRINTING OF THE WORDS 'TRICK OR TREAT' DID NOT OCCUR UNTIL 1934, WHEN A NEWSPAPER DISCUSSED THE PRANKS OF CHILDREN IN OREGON AND THE TROUBLE THEY CAUSED POLICE.]

[*No.* 55–57
EARLY HALLOWEEN
PHOTOGRAPHS.]

[*Nº.* 58–59 WITCHES ARRIVE IN THE 20ᵀᴴ CENTURY.]

 N°· 60 ROOSEVELT ERA, WORKS PROGRESS ADMINISTRATION (WPA) POSTER.

[*N⁰.* 61 WPA POSTER.]

[*N⁰.* 62 BY THE 1940s, 'TRICK OR TREATING' HAD BECOME
WIDESPREAD, REPLACING THE EARLIER PRACTICE
OF POSTCARD EXCHANGE. BOOK, FILM, AND TV
PROMOTION HAS SINCE HELPED MAKE HALLOWEEN
THE 2ND MOST POPULAR HOLIDAY IN THE U.S.]

NOTES &
Sources

Page 19. Image No. 19. c. 1903. *Fred R. Hamlin's Musical Extravaganza: The Wizard of Oz.* The U.S. Lithograph Co., Russell-Morgan Print, Cincinnati & New York. (poster, lithograph, color, 105 x 70 cm)

Page 20. Image No. 20. c. 1902. *The Witch House, Salem, Mass.* Cosmos Pictures Co., New York, No. 2452. (photomechanical print, halftone)

Page 20. Image No. 21. c. 1856–1907. *Haunted Castle.* Published by Currier & Ives, New York. (print, lithograph, hand-colored)

Page 21–28. Image No. 22–31. Halloween postcards courtesy of Lisa Morton.

Page 28. Image No. 32. c. 1898. *The Haunted Lane.* Melander. (photographic print on stereo card, stereograph)

Page 29. Image No. 33. *Raising a Ghost by The Magic Lantern.* From Houdini collection, Library of Congress. (print, engraving)

Page 29. Image No. 34. c. 1920–1930. *Houdini and the Ghost of Abraham Lincoln.* (slide, lantern) SUMMARY: Was that a spirit or a double exposure? Harry Price was a member of the Society for Psychical Research, Librarian of the Magicians' Club of London and a member of the Society of American Magicians when, in 1922, his article "Cold Light on Spiritualistic Phenomena" was published in the *Journal of the Society for Psychical Research.* Houdini valued this expose of how a photographer could produce fraudulent "spirit photographs" that purportedly documented the apparition and social interaction of figures from beyond. Demonstrating the company he could keep if the right technique were employed Houdini had himself photographed with the ghost of Abraham Lincoln."

Page 30. Image No. 35. Halloween postcard courtesy of Lisa Morton.

Relationships

Pages 31–37. Image No. 36–42. Halloween postcards courtesy of Lisa Morton.

Community and Children

Page 38–39. Image No. 43–44. Halloween postcards courtesy of Lisa Morton.

Page 39. Image No. 45. c. 1917. *Halloween.* (photographic print)

Page 40–41. Image No. 46–47. Halloween postcards courtesy of Lisa Morton.

WWI Era

Page 42. Image No. 48. c. 1919. *War Gardens Over the Top. The Seeds of Victory Insure the Fruits of Peace.* Maginel Wright Enright. National War Garden Commission, funder/sponsor, Washington, D.C. (print, poster, color, 74 x 57 cm)

Page 43. Image No. 49. *Eat Less and Let Us Be Thankful That We Have Enough to Share 2ith Those Who Fight for Freedom.* A. Hendee. Edwards & Deutsch Litho. Co., Chicago. (print, poster, lithograph, color, 73 x 54 cm)

1920s and Beyond

Page 44. Image No. 50. Halloween postcard courtesy of Lisa Morton.

Page 45. Image No. 51. c. 1869. *Bird's-Eye View of Anoka, Anoka County, Minnesota. Drawn by A. Ruger.* Chicago, Merchant's Lithographing Co., (colored map 39 x 51 cm)

Page 45–47. Image No. 52–54. Halloween postcards courtesy of Lisa Morton.

Page 48. Image No. 55–56. Halloween photographs. Flickr.com, Creative Commons.

Page 48. Image No. 57. c. 1920s. *Not a Modern Witches' Council—but Members of [The Holy and Undivided Trinity of Castle Rising, Norfolk, England].* (photographic print).

Page 49. Image No. 58. Halloween postcard. riptheskull, Flickr.com, Creative Commons.

Page 49. Image No. 59. c. 1909–1910. *Halloween—Ancient and Modern.* Berryman (C.K.), No. 1131. Washington Star. (drawing)

Page 50. Image No. 60. c. 1936–1941. *"Hansel and Gretel," The Gingerbread Children, by Humperdinck Music, Animals, Dancing, Songs.* Massachusetts Federal Art Project. Work Projects Administration Poster Collection, Library of Congress. (poster, silkscreen, color)

Page 51. Image No. 61. c. 1936. *Halloween Roller Skating Carnival on the Mall, Central Park. Bring Your Skates. Come In Costume. Prizes Will Be Given For Costumes.* Federal Art Project, WPA. New York. (print on board, poster, silkscreen, color)

Page 52. Image No. 62. c. 1936–1940. *October's Bright Blue Weather: A Good Time to Read!* Chicago, Illinois, WPA Art Project. (print on board, poster, silkscreen, color)

CPSIA information can be obtained
at www.ICGtesting.com
Printed in the USA
LVIC04n1445040614
388612LV00010B/53